Somerset's Lost Railways

by
Peter Dale

Engines, nos. 40564 (a Midland 2P 4-4-0) and 53810 (a Somerset & Dorset Railway 2-8-0), passing Radstock. The town's brewery is in the background.

First published in the United Kingdom, 2001,
by Stenlake Publishing,
Telephone / Fax: 01290 551122

ISBN 1 84033 171 2

ACKNOWLEDGEMENTS

I would like to thank my father for introducing me to this absorbing hobby and Ken Jones for introducing me to this project. The publishers wish to thank the following for contributing pictures to this book: John Alsop for the front cover, inside front cover, pages 2–4, 6, 8–12, 14, 15, 19–24, 27–48, the inside back cover and the back cover; the Rev. D.J. Lane for pages 16 and 25; D.P. Leckonby for page 13; W.A.C. Smith for pages 7 and 18; and Neville Stead for pages 1 and 5.

The Midland Station at Bath.

INTRODUCTION

Four major companies played a part in the development of Somerset's railways. The Great Western Railway (GWR) was the largest of these and many of its lines in the west of England (and those of its associated companies) were built to a broad gauge of seven feet (often given as 7 feet ¼ inch). Britain's rail system today uses a standard gauge of 4 feet 8 ½ inch and although it has been in use since the earliest days of railways it was not always certain that it would become the standard – indeed in many other countries a different gauge is the norm. The difference in gauge meant that trains could not run on different companies' tracks and passengers and goods had to be trans-shipped from one to the other. After investigations by a Gauge Commission the GWR had to give up the broad gauge for the narrow one, but the broad gauge stretched north to Wolverhampton and west to Penzance and it did not finally disappear until May 1892.

The other major railways in Somerset were the Midland Railway, the London & South Western Railway (LSWR) and the Somerset & Dorset Railways. In the years leading up to 1923 there was a process of consolidation by which smaller companies were absorbed by larger ones (the Somerset & Dorset was taken over jointly by the Midland and LSWR) but in 1922 there were still well over a hundred different companies in Britain. In 1923 there was a major shift when all but a few minor companies were grouped into four larger concerns by an Act of Parliament. They were the GWR (which continued in an enlarged form), the Southern Railway (which included the LSWR), the London, Midland & Scottish Railway (LMS – which included the Midland) and the London & North Eastern Railway (LNER). These four companies continued until nationalisation in 1948.

Both the GWR's original route via Bristol to Exeter and the west, and its later (1906), shorter, route via Castle Cary (from Reading to Taunton) cross the county, while the LSWR route from London to Exeter runs along the Somerset–Dorset border. In the east the Midland Railway made an incursion as far as Bath, but played a far greater role in the history of Somerset's railways as a joint owner of the Somerset & Dorset Joint Railway. This line (known as the 'Slow and Dirty' to its detractors and the 'Swift and Delightful' to its admirers), with its main line from Bath to Bournemouth and branches to Wells, Bridgwater and Highbridge, was second only to the GWR in importance in Somerset. It retained many of its independent features as a joint line following the grouping as its owners, the Midland and the LSWR, were constituents of different groups.

The earliest public railway in Somerset was part of the Bristol & Exeter Railway as it opened its main line in sections, the first of which was from Bristol to Bridgwater on 14 June 1841, shortly before the GWR opened its main line from London to Bristol. The Bristol & Exeter was initially leased by the GWR, but in May 1849 took over operation of the line itself until it later became part of the GWR in 1876.

It is hoped that this book will provide pleasant memories of travel in a slower age, before the advent of motorways, and the attendant problems of congestion, pollution and road rage, and perhaps also it will stimulate interest in readers to see what is left of Britain's railway heritage.

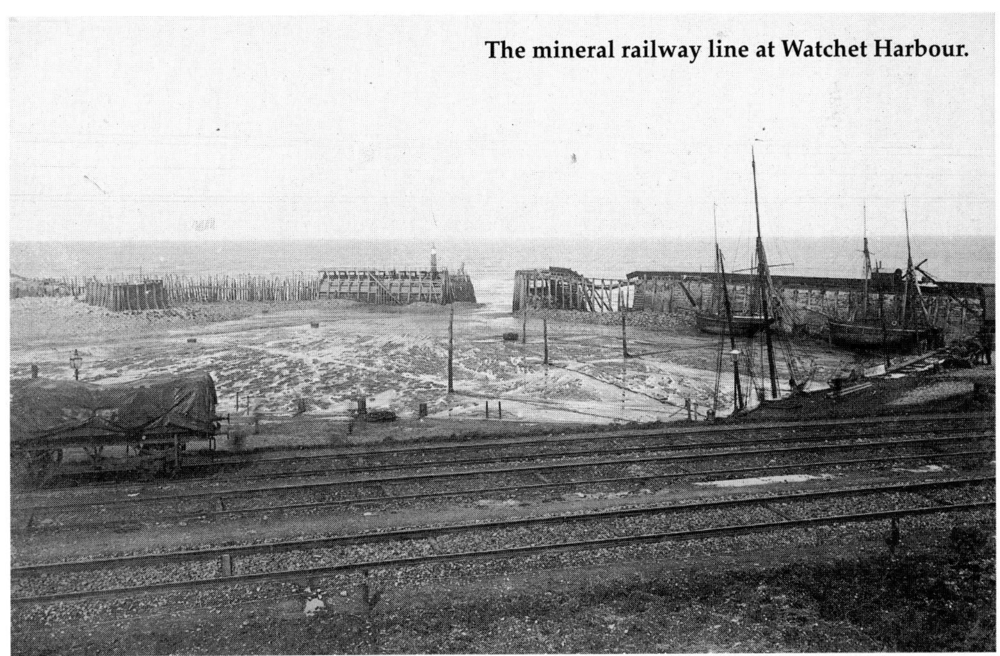

The mineral railway line at Watchet Harbour.

Somerset & Dorset Railway *

Passenger service withdrawn	7 March 1966
Distance	58.5 miles (Corfe Mullen Junction to Burnham)
Company	Somerset & Dorset Railway

Stations closed	*Date*
Henstridge	7 March 1966
Templecombe Lower Platform	3 January 1966
Wincanton	7 March 1966
Cole	7 March 1966
Evercreech Junction	7 March 1966
Pylle	7 March 1966
West Pennard	7 March 1966
Glastonbury and Street	7 March 1966
Ashcott	7 March 1966
Shapwick	7 March 1966
Edington Burtle **	7 March 1966
Bason Bridge	7 March 1966
Highbridge East ***	7 March 1966
Burnham-On-Sea	29 October 1951

Henstridge Station, the smallest station on the line, looking towards Templecombe.

* The closed stations on this line that were in Dorset were Stalbridge, Shillingstone, Stourpaine, Blandford, Charlton Marshall, Spetisbury and Bailey Gate.

** Known as Edington Road until July 1890 and Edington Junction until June 1953.

*** Known as Burnham until July 1920.

A Somerset & Dorset 2-8-0, no. 53807, passing Templecombe Lower Station with a service from Birmingham to Bournemouth, Summer 1962.

The Somerset Central Railway was authorised in 1852 to link Highbridge and Glastonbury and opened as a broad gauge line on 28 August 1854, worked by the Bristol & Exeter Railway. From the start it was intended to extend towards the Wilts, Somerset & Weymouth Railway which the GWR had taken over in 1850. Early on the railway was described as 'going from nowhere to nowhere over a turf moor' and extensions to Burnham and Wells were authorised in July 1855. The Burnham extension opened in May 1858 and was intended to provide a starting point for a passenger ship service to Wales. Instead of an extension eastwards via Wells to Frome, powers were obtained from Glastonbury towards Bruton on the narrow gauge to link with the Dorset Central Railway, and extend the narrow gauge to Burnham. The Bristol & Exeter opposed and forced the extension of the broad gauge to Bruton but few trains used it. The Bristol & Exeter's lease expired in August 1861 but the Somerset Central was not ready to work the line itself and the Bristol & Exeter continued to work it until 3 February 1862 when the narrow gauge began running. On the same day the Dorset Central opened its extension from Templecombe to Cole and in August the Somerset Central and Dorset Central amalgamated to form the Somerset & Dorset.

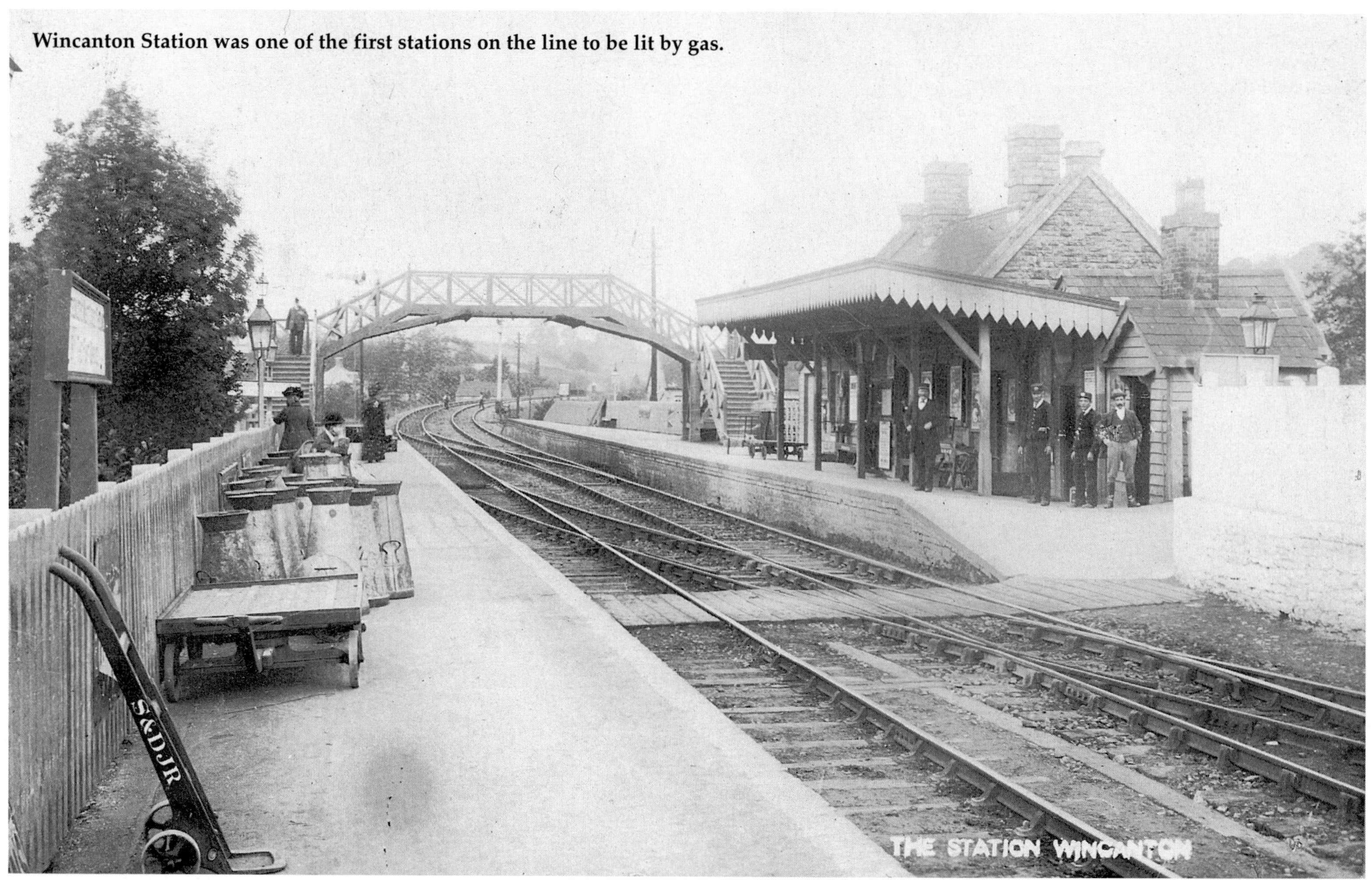

Wincanton Station was one of the first stations on the line to be lit by gas.

It was hoped the line would generate considerable traffic as a route between the English and Bristol Channels, avoiding the long and treacherous passage around Land's End. But this traffic did not materialise and the combined concern was overstretched financially, seeking salvation by changing itself into a north–south link by extending to Bath. After this extension opened in 1874 only the part south of Evercreech Junction was regarded as the main line, while the line to Highbridge and Burnham was relegated to the status of a branch line.

A class 2P 4-4-0, no. 40563, and standard class 5 4-6-0, no. 73051, arrive at Evercreech Junction Station with the 'Pines Express' (the 10.15 a.m. service from Manchester to Bournemouth), 29 August 1958.

Somerset & Dorset Railway (Bath extension)

Passenger service withdrawn	7 March 1966
Distance	26.5 miles (Bath [Midland] to Evercreech Junction South)
Company	Somerset & Dorset Railway

Stations closed	*Date*
Midford	7 March 1966
Wellow	7 March 1966
Shoscombe and Single Hill Halt	7 March 1966
Radstock North *	7 March 1966
Midsomer Norton Upper **	7 March 1966
Chilcompton	7 March 1966
Binegar	7 March 1966
Masbury Halt	7 March 1966
Shepton Mallett Charlton Road ***	7 March 1966
Evercreech New	7 March 1966

Wellow Station. The locomotive appears to be an 0-6-0.

* Known as Radstock until September 1949.

** Known as Midsomer Norton until October 1898 and Midsomer Norton & Welton until September 1949.

*** Known as Shepton Mallett until October 1883.

When the Somerset Central converted to narrow gauge it expected the Bristol & Exeter Railway to lay in a third rail from Highbridge to Bristol and then to allow them running powers through to Bristol. When the Bristol & Exeter refused to go along with this and other links to Bristol were likewise denied, the Somerset & Dorset Railway looked to Bath and a connection to the north via the Midland Railway to solve its financial problems. After the receivers were discharged in 1870, further capital was raised and the Bath extension opened in July 1874 which also gave access to the Somerset coalfield. The traffic levels were good but it was more than the Somerset & Dorset could handle and its rolling stock and track were overstretched. In financial difficulty again a buyer was sought and a first approach was made to the GWR, but when the LSWR's manager heard this he was horrified. He had urgent talks with the Midland's general manager and they promptly made a joint offer to lease the line for 999 years, starting from 1 November 1875. This was accepted and the Somerset & Dorset Joint Railway came into being.

Staff at Radstock Station. The stationmaster is seated in the middle.

The Joint Committee introduced considerable improvements over the next few years with the permanent way under the control of the LSWR and motive power becoming the responsibility of the Midland. As these companies became part of the Southern and the LMS respectively in 1923, the Somerset & Dorset retained many distinctive features, including the royal blue livery which had first been adopted in 1886. The Somerset & Dorset was a useful north – south link with a Bournemouth to Manchester Express and many long distance expresses to the Southern system at summer weekends, although these services presented considerable operating problems over the single track sections. In 1958 the Western Region took over control of the Somerset & Dorset and a long run down began. There was considerable bad feeling over the closure and the replacement express coach service took over three and a half hours to cover the seventy miles from Bath to Bournemouth, when seventy years earlier steam trains had made the journey in just over two hours.

Binegar Station. The Oakhill Brewey brought its stout here on its own 2 feet 6 inch line.

Somerset & Dorset Railway (Wells branch)

Passenger service withdrawn	29 October 1951	*Stations closed*	*Date*
Distance	5.5 miles	Polsham *	29 October 1951
Company	Somerset Central Railway	Wells (Priory Road) **	29 October 1951

Initially it was intended that Wells would be on the Somerset Central main line but when this was extended it veered southwards and the city had to make do with a branch line. This broad gauge branch from Glastonbury opened in March 1859 and was worked by the Bristol & Exeter Railway until August 1861. It became narrow gauge in 1868. In the line's early days there was a daily broad gauge passenger train from Bristol to Wells via Highbridge and a number of through trains from Wells to Highbridge; by 1914 there were ten trains daily but only one worked through to Highbridge. The Somerset & Dorset was the first of three railways to reach Wells; the other two opened as broad gauge lines but they were separated by the Somerset & Dorset. An agreement was reached to allow broad gauge trains over the Somerset & Dorset and a rental was fixed. However, the Board of Trade refused permission for this to happen for reasons of safety, although the Somerset & Dorset still insisted that the rent was due! Not until the broad gauge disappeared at Wells did through running begin.

* Known as Polsham Halt from July 1938.

** Known as Wells until October 1883.

Somerset & Dorset Railway (Bridgwater branch)

Passenger service withdrawn	1 December 1952
Distance	7.3 miles (Edington Junction to Bridgewater)
Company	Bridgwater Railway

Stations closed	*Date*
Cossington	1 December 1952
Bawdrip Halt	1 December 1952
Bridgwater *	1 December 1952

Cossington Station. The large building behind the station was the stationmaster's house.

The Bristol & Exeter Railway opened as far as Bridgwater in June 1841 but local people were not satisfied with the service provided and in 1882, after three earlier attempts, an Act was obtained for an alternative line from Edington Road on the Somerset & Dorset Railway. The railway opened on 21 July 1890 and although it was worked as part of the Somerset & Dorset, it was leased by the LSWR and remained an independent company until it became part of the Southern Railway at the grouping of 1923. At Bridgwater there was an extension, just over half a mile in length, that served the cattle dock and terminated beside the River Parrett, and until the First World War ship-borne freight was unloaded there. In the early days of the line a number of semi-fast trains were run to Templecombe for fast connections to Waterloo to encourage passengers on this route rather than the GWR. There was, in any case, a good service on the branch – up to fourteen daily trains – taking about fifteen minutes for the journey.

* Known as Bridgwater North from 26 September 1949.

Somerset & Dorset Railway (Templecombe branch)

Passenger service withdrawn	7 March 1966	*Stations closed*	*Date*
Distance	0.4 miles	Templecombe Lower	17 January 1887
Company	Salisbury & Yeovil Railway		

At Templecombe the Somerset & Dorset passed under the Salisbury & Yeovil (later LSWR) main line to the west. The original connection allowed trains from Burnham to join the main line towards Waterloo, but trains then had to back down the main line to reach Templecombe (Salisbury & Yeovil) station; some trains also called at the Somerset & Dorset's own station, Templecombe Lower. This arrangement became increasingly difficult to work as traffic grew on both lines. When doubling of the Salisbury & Yeovil line was proposed a new solution had to be found and a short branch was opened in April 1870 from Templecombe (Salisbury & Yeovil) to join the Somerset & Dorset to the north. Somerset & Dorset trains then used the north facing edge of the platform of the Salisbury & Yeovil station, an arrangement resulting in southbound trains having to back out of the station, while northbound trains had to back into it. Templecombe Lower Platform, to the south, replaced the original Somerset & Dorset station, Templecombe Lower, in January 1887.

Midland Railway to Bath *

Passenger service withdrawn	7 March 1966
Distance	10 miles
Company	Midland Railway

Stations closed	*Date*
Kelston for Saltwood	1 January 1949
Weston (Bath) **	21 September 1953
Bath Green Park ***	7 March 1966

A Somerset & Dorset 2-8-0 with a long freight train on the Midland Railway at Bath. The structure on the front bufferbeam was used to make detailed measurements of the locomotive's performance. This may indicate that the picture was taken just after this type was introduced in 1914.

* Closed stations on this line that were in Gloucestershire were Bitton and Warmley.
** Known as Weston until October 1934.
*** Known as Bath until June 1951 (the name Bath Queen Square was unofficial).

Engine no. 44559 leaving Bath Green Park with a service to Templecombe, 15 August 1962.

In order to reach Bristol and to prevent the broad gauge from extending into its territory, the Midland Railway took over the Bristol & Gloucester Railway in 1845, the irony being that they then had to operate broad gauge trains for a while until they converted it to narrow gauge. The line to Bath was built by the Midland Railway as a branch from Mangotsfield and despite having been first proposed in 1846 was not authorised until 1864. It opened on 4 August 1869. Passengers were encouraged by the provision of excursion trains but not everyone liked the newcomer and a complaint was made in 1870 about the night-time whistling of locomotives in the station. For the opening the Midland built a very impressive station in Bath which really came into its own when the Somerset & Dorset Railway's trains began running into Bath in July 1874 and provided the Midland with a route to the south and west. Subsequently, Bath Midland (renamed Bath Green Park in 1951) was associated with the Somerset & Dorset rather than the Midland whose property it was. The line closed in March 1966, losing its raison d'être when the Somerset & Dorset was closed. Subsequently part of the line in Gloucestershire has been reopened as a preserved line based on Bitton Station and known as the Avon Valley Railway.

Chard branch (LSWR)

Passenger service withdrawn	10 September 1962	*Stations closed*	*Date*
Distance	3.1 miles	Chard Town	1 January 1917
Company	Chard Railway		

Chard got its first railway link in May 1863, having been disappointed in its hopes to be on a main line. This line ran from Chard Road, later Chard Junction, on the LSWR main line and was absorbed by the LSWR in 1864. The Chard Railway also had powers to connect to the Chard Canal and these were later used to provide a connection to the line from Taunton at Chard Joint (a forty-one chain length of track was also joint property), although separate staffs and signalboxes were maintained there for many years. The LSWR's own station, Chard Town, was closed on 1 January 1917 in the interests of economy when the GWR took over operation of trains from Chard Joint to Chard Junction.

Chard branch (GWR)

Passenger service withdrawn	10 September 1962	*Stations closed*	*Date*
Distance	12.8 miles	Hatch	10 September 1962
Company	Bristol & Exeter Railway	Ilton Halt	10 September 1962
		Ilminster	10 September 1962
Stations closed	*Date*	Donyatt Halt	10 September 1962
Thornfalcon *	10 September 1962	Chard Central **	10 September 1962

Thornfalcon Station was not opened until 1871.

* Known as Thorne until 1 January 1902 and Thorne Falcon until July 1890.

** Known as Chard Joint until February 1928 and Chard until 26 September 1949.

Hatch Station at the village of Hatch Beauchamp was one of the branch's original stations and was more typical of the Bristol & Exeter railway then Thornfalcon.

Despite the connection to the LSWR main line the people of Chard were not satisfied with a railway that linked them to Devon and Dorset and continued to look for a connection to the county town, Taunton, and the rest of the county to the north. The earliest proposal for a railway to the north was made in 1830, but a canal was built instead. During the Railway Mania of 1845 the Bristol & English Channels Direct Junction Railway was proposed and would have passed through Chard. However, nothing came of this or a rival proposal by two canal companies. The Chard & Taunton Railway was incorporated in 1861 but being unable to raise the money it was taken over by the Bristol & Exeter.

An ex-GWR Pannier Tank with a service from Chard Junction at Chard Central, July 1959.

The line ran from Creech Junction on the Bristol & Exeter main line and opened as a broad gauge line in September 1866, although goods traffic did not start until March the following year when the goods shed was completed. At this time the Joint station had bay platforms at each end as through running was not possible due to the break of gauge. In 1878 it was proposed that the broad gauge branches between Bristol and Exeter be converted to standard gauge and this was done so that by mid-1884 the Chard branch was the only broad gauge branch line east of Exeter. It was left like this as it was feared that if it was converted the LSWR would demand running powers to Taunton. It was not converted until Sunday 19 July 1891.

Devon & Somerset Railway *

Passenger service withdrawn	3 October 1966
Distance	42.6 miles
Company	Devon & Somerset Railway

Stations closed	*Date*
Milverton	3 October 1966
Wiveliscombe	3 October 1966
Venn Cross	3 October 1966
Dulverton	3 October 1966

Milverton Station. The goods shed is to the left at the end of the platform while the goods yard is in the middle distance.

* Closed stations on this line that were in Devon were Morebath, Morebath Junction Halt, East Anstey, Yeo Mill Halt, Bishop's Nympton & Molland, South Molton, Filleigh, Swimbridge, and Barnstaple (renamed Barnstaple Victoria Road in 1949).

A class 3MT 2-6-2T, no. 82044, at Dulverton with an 11.00 a.m. from Barnstaple Junction to Taunton, 6 June 1964.

This broad gauge line to Barnstaple was opened from a junction at Norton Fitzwarren in November 1873 (the gauge was narrowed in May 1881) and was leased by the Bristol & Exeter Railway from the Devon & Somerset until it was taken over by the GWR in 1901. During construction there were many financial difficulties and when supplies ran out a party of seventy armed navvies marched on Wiveliscombe. The initial train service was very poor, but the line was the GWR's route to both Barnstaple and Ilfracombe and services were improved after installation of crossing loops at Morebath, East Anstey, and Bishop's Nympton & Molland. In the 1930s the section from Norton Fitzwarren to Milverton was doubled. The Cornish Riviera Express carried a slip coach for Ilfracombe that was slipped at Taunton and worked over the line, while the 9.00 a.m. from Paddington carried a restaurant car that worked to Barnstaple. The GWR route to Barnstaple was considerably shorter than the Southern Railway's route from Waterloo – in 1939 the journey time from Paddington to Barnstaple was four hours and thirty-five minutes, compared to five hours exactly by the Southern's Atlantic Coast Express. There appeared to be a deliberate policy to run the line down in the 1960s in favour of the Southern route. Freight was diverted to it and even passenger trains via Taunton to Ilfracombe were made to go through Exeter.

Taunton – Minehead branch

Passenger service withdrawn	4 January 1971
Distance	22.8 miles (Norton Fitzwarren to Minehead)
Company	West Somerset/Minehead Railways

Stations closed	*Date*
Bishop's Lydeard	4 January 1971
Crowcombe *	4 January 1971
Stogumber	4 January 1971
Williton	4 January 1971
Watchet	4 January 1971
Washford **	4 January 1971
Blue Anchor	4 January 1971
Dunster	4 January 1971
Minehead	4 January 1971

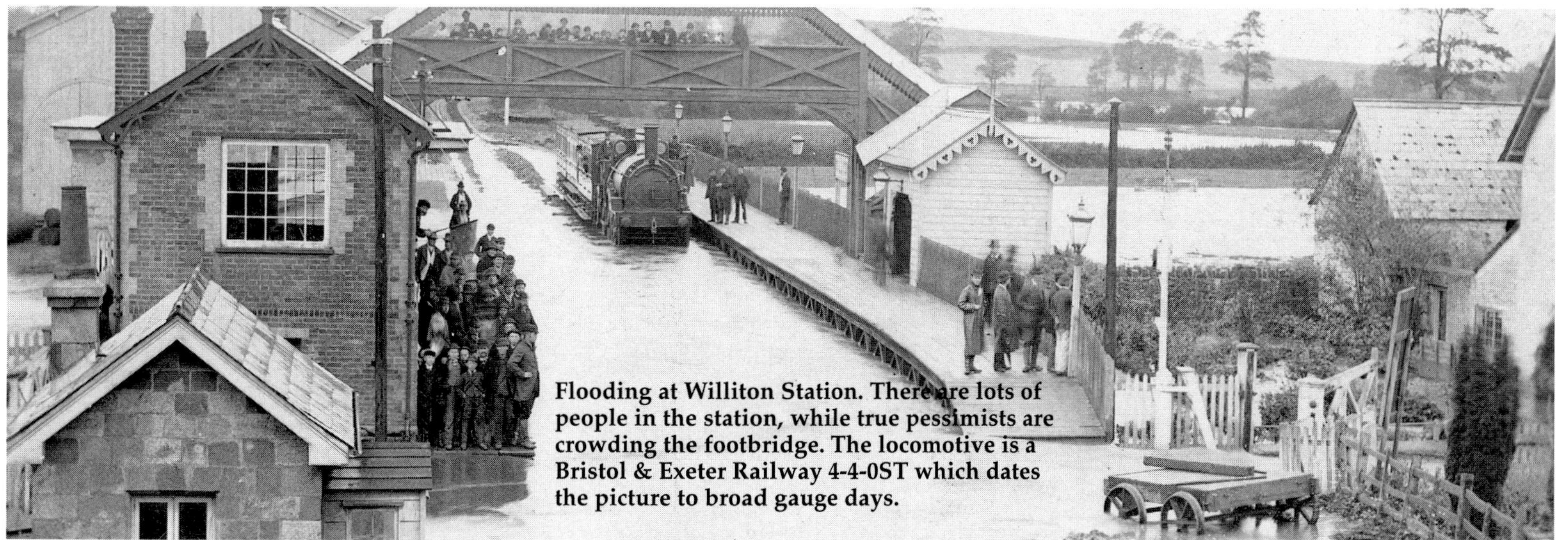

Flooding at Williton Station. There are lots of people in the station, while true pessimists are crowding the footbridge. The locomotive is a Bristol & Exeter Railway 4-4-0ST which dates the picture to broad gauge days.

The West Somerset Railway was opened from the Bristol & Exeter Railway main line west of Taunton to Watchet in March 1862 as a broad gauge line. It was leased to the Bristol & Exeter Railway in perpetuity, the West Somerset Company existing until 1922. Trains ran from Taunton, there being no station at the junction when the line opened. The Minehead Railway was authorised in 1871 to build the extension to Minehead and was opened in July 1874, again worked by the Bristol & Exeter and absorbed by the GWR in 1897. The gauge was converted in October 1882. In 1934 the section from Minehead to Dunster was doubled, followed by the Norton Fitzwarren to Bishop's Lydeard section in 1936. Despite this the usual rundown in traffic occurred in the 1950s and 60s. After British Railways closed the line a new West Somerset Railway was formed as a preserved line which reopened in 1976 from Minehead to Blue Anchor and to Bishop's Lydeard in 1979. A new halt has been opened at Doniford Beach and a day on the line is well worthwhile for holidaymakers in the area, giving an opportunity to see something of a bygone era.

* Known as Crowcombe Heathfield until December 1889.

** Sometimes known as Washford for Cleeve Abbey.

An 0-6-0, no. 2467, at Minehead Station.

Weston-super-Mare branch

Passenger service withdrawn	1 March 1884	*Stations closed*	*Date*
Distance	1.5 miles	Weston-super-Mare	20 July 1866
Company	Bristol & Exeter Railway	Weston-super-Mare *	1 March 1884

The branch from Weston Junction to Weston-super-Mare opened on 14 June 1841. Weston did not want a main line railway when the Bristol & Exeter was built and the first passengers arrived in rail coaches drawn by three horses. Other than a morning through train to Bristol and an evening return, the branch remained horse worked until April 1851. The line became mixed gauge in 1875. On 1 March 1884 the present Weston loop opened to the standard gauge and the branch closed.

* This station replaced the original Bristol & Exeter station.

Clevedon branch

Passenger service withdrawn	3 October 1966	*Stations closed*	*Date*
Distance	3.6 miles	Clevedon	3 October 1966
Company	Bristol & Exeter Railway		

The Bristol & Exeter Railway was authorised in 1845 to build this branch as a broad gauge line. It opened on 28 July 1847 and was worked by the GWR until May 1849 when the Bristol & Exeter took over the running of trains. The branch was converted to the narrow gauge in September 1879 and later there was a siding at Clevedon which made a connection with the Weston, Clevedon & Portishead Railway. There was an intensive shuttle service of about twenty trains per day in the 1920s, operated by railmotors until 1935 when these were replaced by autotrains (around 1850 the line was at times worked by the Bristol & Exeter Railway's pioneer steam railmotor, 'Fairfield'). In addition a daily through coach ran to Bristol between 1924 and 1936. This left Clevedon at 8.47 a.m. and left Bristol on the return at 5.15 p.m., being slipped at Yatton and worked in to Clevedon by the branch train; later a through train left Bristol at 1.10 p.m. and returned from Clevedon at 2.17 p.m. There was also a daily goods train.

Portishead branch

Passenger service withdrawn	7 September 1964
Distance	9.6 miles (Portishead Junction to Portishead)
Company	Bristol & Portishead Pier and Railway

Stations closed	*Date*
Ashton Gate Halt *	7 September 1964
Clifton Bridge	7 September 1964
Nightingale Valley Halt	12 September 1932
Ham Green Halt	7 September 1964
Pill	7 September 1964
Portbury Shipyard	26 March 1923
Portbury	30 April 1962
Portishead **	7 September 1964

* Known as Ashton Gate Platform until August 1928 and then Ashton Gate until 29 October 1962. This station was closed between 1917 and May 1926. After the withdrawal of passenger services it was used for football excursions between 1970 and 1977.

** This station replaced an earlier one four hundred metres north in January 1954, when a power station was built on the site of the earlier one.

Ashton Gate Halt. The branch is on the left while the lines on the right lead to the harbour line and Canon's Marsh Goods Depot

Clifton Bridge Station. Brunel's bridge across the Avon is in the background. It was begun in 1836 and finished as a monument to him in 1864, five years after his death.

The earliest proposal for a railway to Portishead was for a colliery line that would have been gravity worked, i.e. the loaded wagons going down the line were to have hauled the empty ones back up by means of a rope and pulley. Later, the great engineer, Brunel, proposed a line worked on a system whereby trains would be powered by atmospheric pressure. In the event, it opened as a conventional broad gauge line from a junction with the Bristol & Exeter Railway, which worked the line, in April 1867. The following year an extension to the pier was opened. The line was converted to narrow gauge in January 1880; the Bristol & Exeter had become part of the GWR in 1876. There were no crossing places until 1880 when a loop was installed at Clifton Bridge and in 1883 the line was doubled as far as there. Trains were worked to and from Bristol Temple Meads and from 1929 a half hourly service was introduced. The line is still open for freight traffic.

GWR (Wells branch)

Passenger service withdrawn	9 September 1963
Distance	31.5 miles
Company	East Somerset Railway/Bristol & Exeter Railway

Stations closed	*Date*
Congresbury	9 September 1963
Sandford & Banwell	9 September 1963
Winscombe	9 September 1963
Axbridge	9 September 1963
Cheddar	9 September 1963

Stations closed	*Date*
Draycott	9 September 1963
Lodge Hill	9 September 1963
Wookey	9 September 1963
Wells *	9 September 1963
Wells **	1 January 1878
Shepton Mallet ***	9 September 1963
Cranmore	9 September 1963
Wanstrow	9 September 1963

The station building in this view of Winscombe replaced a wooden structure in 1905.

* Known as Wells Tucker Street between July 1920 and May 1950.
** This was the East Somerset Railway Station that closed when running began between the two lines.

*** Known as Shepton Mallet High Street from 26 September 1949.

Cheddar Station was provided with an overall roof, an indication of the town's status.

The GWR line from Yatton (on the Taunton to Bristol line) to Witham (on the West of England main line) ran through Wells and Cheddar. It was built in two parts. The East Somerset Railway opened its broad gauge line from Witham to Shepton Mallet in November 1858 (extended to Wells on 1 March 1862) and this was worked by the GWR from the outset. Meanwhile the line from Yatton to Wells was originally to be built by the Somerset & Dorset Railway as the Cheddar Valley & Yatton Railway, but ended up being built by the Bristol & Exeter following an agreement with the Somerset & Dorset. The broad gauge line was opened to Cheddar on 3 August 1869 and to Wells on 5 April 1870.

No. 5554 leaving Wells, June 1959.

It had been intended that the line would be extended to a junction with the Somerset & Dorset and, by means of running powers for nine chains, link with the East Somerset and use its station. However, the Board of Trade would not agree to this. So Wells, the smallest city in England, had three stations. The two broad gauge ones were separated by the Somerset & Dorset which had become narrow gauge in 1868, and it was not until 1877, when both broad gauge lines had been narrowed, that the connection could be used. Despite having run through it for over fifty years GWR trains did not call at the Somerset & Dorset station, Priory Road, until October 1934. Trains over the whole line took about two hours and in season it carried considerable strawberry traffic. Stone trains still run to the quarries at Merehead while at Cranmore the artist, David Shepherd, has established a preservation centre known as the East Somerset Railway.

Shepton Mallet Station. On the left is an 0-6-0ST, a type which preceded the ubiquitous GWR Pannier Tank.

Wrington Vale Light Railway

		Stations closed	Date
Passenger service withdrawn	14 September 1931	Wrington	14 September 1931
Distance	6.5 miles	Langford	14 September 1931
Company	Great Western Railway	Burrington	14 September 1931
		Blagdon	14 September 1931

Langford Station. The line's origins as a light railway are shown by the flat bottom rail.

Early proposals to build a railway through the Chew Valley came to nothing but the area has rich farming land and a Light Railway Order was granted in March 1898. This coincided with the construction of a large reservoir at Blagdon by the Bristol Waterworks which supported the proposals. The support of the GWR was of far greater importance and it financed and constructed the line, which commenced at Congresbury on its Yatton to Wells branch. Once the line opened in December 1901 it was worked by the GWR and in many ways appeared to be just another GWR branch line. There was however an axleload restriction of fourteen tons which meant that the type of locomotives that could be used were limited and at one time the GWR built a special oil-fired 0-4-0T for it at Swindon. This was withdrawn in 1911, having spent all its working life shunting around Swindon. Instead 0-4-2Ts and, at times, 2-4-0Ts, were used, but in the 1920s one of the four daily trains was a steam railmotor. Occasionally trains terminated at Congresbury but most ran through to Yatton. There was a siding about half a mile before Blagdon Station to the Bristol waterworks yard. Goods traffic continued after passenger services had ceased and the line did not close completely until June 1963.

Bristol – Frome

Passenger service withdrawn	2 November 1959
Distance	23.5 miles (Bristol {North Somerset Junction} to Frome)
Company	Bristol & North Somerset/GWR

Stations closed	*Date*
Brislington	2 November 1959
Whitchurch	2 November 1959
Pensford	2 November 1959
Clutton	2 November 1959
Hallatrow	2 November 1959
Farrington Gurney Halt	2 November 1959
Midsomer Norton & Welton *	2 November 1959
Radstock West **	2 November 1959
Mells Road Halt ***	2 November 1959

Hallatrow Station, looking north. The original station is on the right, while the platform and passing loop on the left were installed in 1909. A footbridge was built later.

This line was built in two sections. The first (southern) part opened in November 1854 as a broad gauge colliery line from a junction with the Wilts, Somerset & Weymouth line at Frome to serve the Somerset coalfield as far as Radstock. The second section, from Bristol to Radstock, was built by the Bristol & North Somerset Railway. It was first authorised in 1863 but due to financial difficulties did not open until September 1873 and was worked by the GWR. The Bristol & North Somerset Railway became part of the GWR in 1884. At first there was a change of gauge at Radstock but in June 1874 the colliery line was converted to narrow gauge. Until July 1875 passengers were carried only on the second section. The halt at Farrington Gurney was very basic and the booking office was a window set into the wall of the Miner's Arms pub. Passenger traffic was never heavy but there were collieries at Pensford, Clutton, Farrington Gurney, Midsomer Norton, Radstock and Mells. Coal had been mined in the Mendip Hills since Roman times and by the turn of the century nearly one and a half million tons per year were being produced. For a while coal traffic continued after the passenger service had been withdrawn but now only part of the southern section sees regular roadstone traffic from Frome to Whatley Quarry.

* Known as Welton until 2 May 1898 and Welton & Midsomer Norton until 1 May 1904.

** Known as Radstock until 26 September 1949.

*** Known as Mells until 16 November 1898 and Mells Road until 17 September 1956.

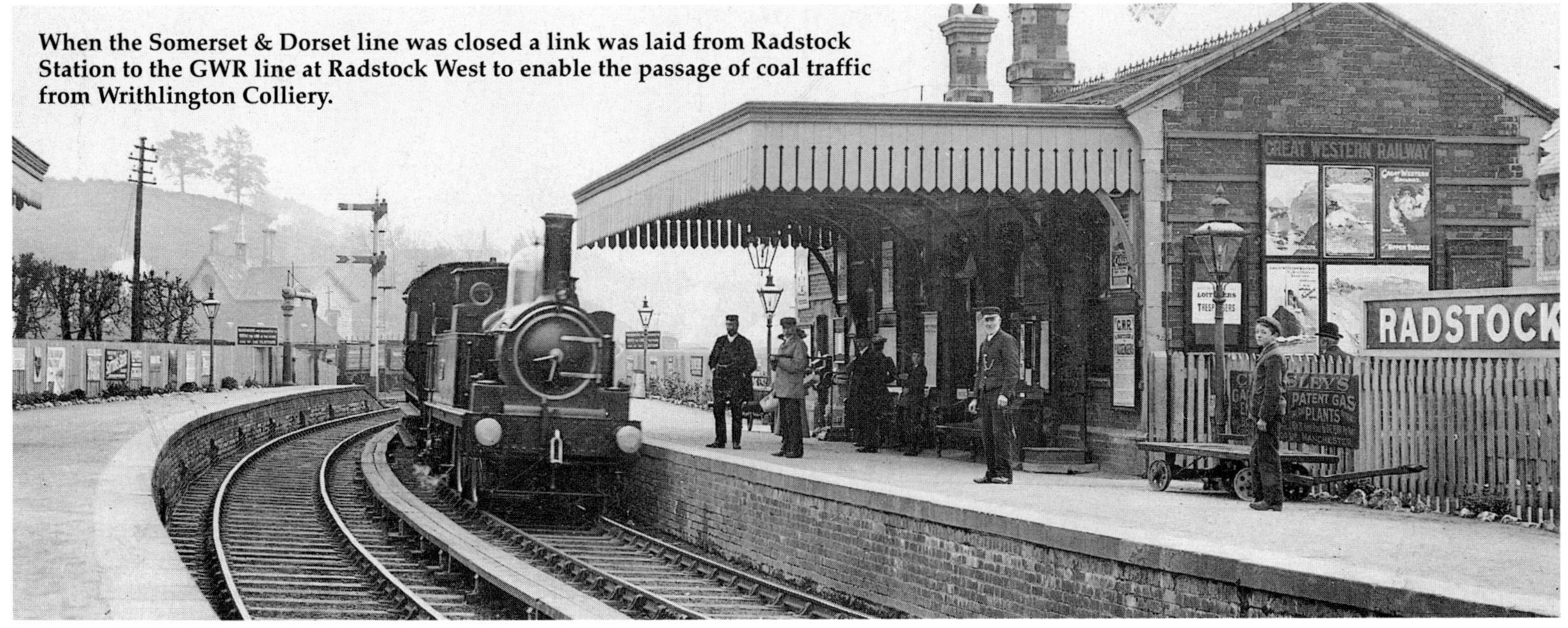

When the Somerset & Dorset line was closed a link was laid from Radstock Station to the GWR line at Radstock West to enable the passage of coal traffic from Writhlington Colliery.

Limpley Stoke – Hallatrow

Passenger service withdrawn	21 September 1925
Distance	11.4 miles
Company	Bristol & North Somerset/Great Western Railway

Stations closed	*Date*
Paulton Halt	21 September 1925
Radford & Timsbury Halt	21 September 1925
Camerton	21 September 1925
Dunkerton Colliery Halt	21 September 1925
Dunkerton	21 September 1925
Combe Hay Halt	21 September 1925
Midford Halt	22 March 1915
Monkton Combe	21 September 1925

This line was built to assist the exploitation of the Somerset coalfield. The first section was built by the Bristol & North Somerset Railway and opened, from a junction at Hallatrow, to Camerton in March 1882. The second section was authorised in 1904 and built along part of the Somerset Coal Canal which the GWR had bought and then obtained an Abandonment Act for. The line opened for passenger traffic through to Limpley Stoke, on the Bath–Weymouth line, in May 1910. Mineral traffic was quite heavy as the line served several collieries and the Cloud Hill Quarry. There were five daily passenger trains each way but all passenger services were withdrawn in March 1915 as an economy measure and not reinstated until July 1923, although Midford Halt remained closed. Despite the line's early closure to passengers, freight services continued and the line did not close completely until February 1951. It is, however, known to thousands of people who never travelled on it as the line featured in *The Ghost Train*, filmed in 1935 at Camerton and Dunkerton; in 1952 *The Titfield Thunderbolt* was also made on the line with Monkton Combe featuring as Titfield.

Yeovil branch

Passenger service withdrawn	5 October 1964
Distance:	20.4 miles (Durston – Yeovil Pen Mill)
Company	Bristol & Exeter Railway

Stations closed	*Date*
Lyng Halt	15 June 1964
Langport West *	15 June 1964
Martock	15 June 1964
Montacute	15 June 1964
Hendford Halt **	15 June 1964
Yeovil (Hendford)	1 June 1861

Langport West Station during a flood of December 1910.

* Known as Langport until July 1906.

** This opened to the west of the original Hendford station in May 1932.

Montacute Station opened in 1882. Opposite the platform is a post with staff collecting equipment.

The Taunton–Yeovil branch of the Bristol & Exeter Railway was authorised in 1845 and while the Yeovil–Martock section was completed in 1849, little more was done until 1852 due to a shortage of finance. The line opened in October 1853 to Yeovil (Hendford) and was extended to the GWR line at Pen Mill in 1857. When the LSWR arrived at Yeovil a new joint station (Yeovil Town) was built and Hendford was closed. The line was initially broad gauge but to forestall a Somerset & Dorset encroachment a third rail was laid in 1867 and a narrow gauge goods train ran from Yeovil to Bridgwater daily, although narrow gauge passenger services did not begin for another year (November 1868). Broad gauge trains were withdrawn at the end of June 1879. The line was not allowed the quiet existence of many branches as in 1906 the new direct line to the west completed its final link by rebuilding the four mile section from Curry Rivel Junction to Athelney to main line standards, and from Athelney a new loop was built to Cogload Junction on the existing main line. This new direct line went a long way to removing the slur that GWR stood for 'Great Way Round' and made the rail distance to Taunton and all points west twenty and a quarter miles less than the old route via Bristol. Branch trains continued to run over the old route from Taunton via Durston to Yeovil (Town) and in the 1920s there were seven daily trains but no Sunday service.

Yeovil Junction – Yeovil Town

Passenger service withdrawn	3 October 1966	*Stations closed*	*Date*
Distance	1.8 miles	Yeovil Town	3 October 1966
Company	Salisbury & Yeovil Railway		

To the right of this view of Yeovil Town Station is the LSWR locomotive shed. The overall roofs were later replaced by platform awnings.

When the Salisbury & Yeovil Railway arrived at Yeovil in 1860 a narrow gauge line was laid beside the Bristol & Exeter branch to Yeovil (Hendford) Station which was used by LSWR passengers and goods until the new joint station, Yeovil Town, was opened on 1 June 1861. Yeovil Junction was built when the Yeovil to Exeter section of the LSWR main line opened and is in Dorset, as is most of this line. There was an intensive service between the Junction and Town stations to connect with most of the main line Southern services, and some services also ran between Yeovil Town and Pen Mill. The Salisbury & Yeovil became part of the LSWR in 1878. After Yeovil Town closed a service operated from Junction to Pen Mill until May 1968.

Weston, Clevedon & Portishead Railway

Passenger service withdrawn	20 May 1940
Distance	14.3 miles
Company	Weston-super–Mare, Clevedon & Portishead Tramways

Stations closed	*Date*
Weston-super-Mare Ashcombe Road	20 May 1940
Milton Road	20 May 1940
Bristol Road	20 May 1940
Ebdon Lane	20 May 1940
Wick St Lawrence	20 May 1940
Ham Lane	20 May 1940
Broadstone	20 May 1940

Stations closed	*Date*
Kingston Road	20 May 1940
Colehouse Lane	20 May 1940
Clevedon	20 May 1940
Clevedon East	20 May 1940
Clevedon All Saints	20 May 1940
Walton Park	20 May 1940
Walton-in-Gordano	20 May 1940
Cadbury Road	20 May 1940
Clapton Road	20 May 1940
Portishead South Portbury Road	20 May 1940
Portishead	20 May 1940

The Weston, Clevedon & Portishead Light Railway had no less than three locomotives named 'Clevedon'. This is the third of them, built by Dubs in 1879 and bought by the light railway in 1901.

Engine no. 1384 at Portishead. Named 'Hesperus' on the Weston, Clevedon & Portishead Light Railway, this engine was built by Sharp Stewart for the Watlington & Princes Risborough Railway and was given its number when that railway was absorbed by the GWR.

This line was authorised in 1885 and although work began on the Weston to Clevedon section in 1888, it was not completed until 1897 and opened on 1 December that year. In August 1899 the name was changed to the Weston, Clevedon & Portishead Light Railway and the extension to Portishead was opened on 7 August 1907. Before the Portishead section opened, the line was in serious financial trouble and the Excess Insurance Company became its principal creditor. In 1909 the line went into receivership and in 1911 H.F. Stephens took over the management of the line. Stephens (later Colonel Stephens) managed a variety of impecunious railways from his office in Tonbridge. He tried to sell the line to the GWR without success and it was one of a few companies that were not included in the grouping in 1923, being left to struggle on as an independent concern.

0-6-0ST 'Portishead' heads the first train to Portishead on 7 August 1907. This was the line's second locomotive to be so named.

The line did provide a more direct route between Weston and Portishead than the GWR and during the 1920s there were three or four trains per day over the whole line with another four on the Weston to Clevedon section. Traffic declined during the 1930s and the line was not brought under government control when war broke out in 1939. In June 1940, after it had closed, the GWR bought the line, intending to use it for coal storage although this did not happen. The line owned a fascinating collection of motive power while some of its early coaches had a Wild West look about them as they were originally built for a frustrated export order from Argentina.

West Somerset Mineral Railway

Passenger service withdrawn	7 November 1898
Distance	12 miles
Company	West Somerset Mineral Railway

Stations closed	*Date*
Watchet	7 November 1898
Washford	7 November 1898
Roadwater	7 November 1898
Combe Row	7 November 1898
Brendon Hill *	7 November 1898
Langham Hill *	7 November 1898
Gupworthy *	7 November 1898

A trial of automatic train control equipment at Kentsford on the mineral line between Watchet and Washford, 5 July 1912. At this point the mineral railway line ran next to the GWR line to Minehead which is seen in the foreground.

* These stations were open for private use only.

Washford Station. When the line was reopened a former Metropolitan Railway 4-4-0T was obtained to operate it.

Industrial railways are usually outside the scope of this book but this line also conveyed passengers. It was authorised in 1855 to exploit the iron ore deposits of the Brendon Hills and ran from Watchet Harbour to Combe Row at the foot of the hills – which it surmounted by means of a forty-nine chain cable-worked incline of 1 in 4 gradient – and then on to terminate at Gupworthy. It opened to public goods traffic in September 1859, preceding the West Somerset Railway by two and a half years, and was standard gauge. Initially the railway was worked by the Brendon Hills Iron Ore Company, but in 1864 the Ebbw Vale Steel, Iron & Coal Company, which had an interest in the mines, agreed to maintain and work the line for fifty-five and a quarter years, for which it would pay a guaranteed minimum sum of £5,575 per annum to the West Somerset Mineral Railway. Passenger services began on 4 September 1865 with four trains daily between Watchet and Combe Row. Stations were also built above the incline at Brendon Hill, Langham Hill and Gupworthy, but the Board of Trade would not sanction operation of passenger trains on the incline so passengers were carried unofficially up the incline to Brendon Hill at their own risk.

The Metropolitan 4-4-0T at Combe Row Station.

In the 1880s imports of iron ore damaged the local mines to the point where they closed, leaving the railway with nothing but general goods and passengers and by 1892 there were only two trains a day. On 7 November 1898 the line closed entirely, although the Ebbw Vale Company was obliged to pay the guaranteed sum as before. In 1907 an attempt was made to revive the mines and the Somerset Mineral Syndicate leased the section from Watchet to Brendon Hill. This was abortive and the workings were abandoned again two years later. The Watchet end of the line was used to test the Angus system of automatic train control in 1912 and 1913. In 1919 the Ebbw Vale Company must have given a huge sigh of relief when it no longer had to pay the guaranteed sum to the West Somerset Mineral Railway, especially as much of the track had already been lifted to help in the war effort.

Closed passenger stations on lines still open to passengers

Line/service		*Stations closed*	*Date*
	LSWR main line	Milborne Port Halt *	7 March 1966
		Sutton Bingham	31 December 1962
		Chard Junction **	7 March 1966

Sutton Bingham Station.

* Known as Milborne Port until 6 September 1961.

** Known as Chard Road until 8 May 1866.

Line/service **GWR Bristol main line**

Stations closed	*Date*
Wellington	5 October 1964
Norton Fitzwarren	30 October 1961
Creech St Michael Halt	5 October 1964
Durston	5 October 1964
Dunball Halt *	5 October 1964
Brent Knoll	4 January 1971
Bleadon & Uphill	5 October 1964
Weston Junction	1 March 1884
Puxton & Worle **	6 April 1964
St Anne's Park	5 January 1970
Saltford	5 January 1970
Bathampton	3 October 1966

Durston Station opened in October 1853 at the junction of the Yeovil branch.

* Known as Dunball until 6 November 1961.

** Known as Banwell until August 1869, then as Worle until March 1884, and as Puxton until March 1922.

After Bleadon & Uphill Station closed it was used as a railway muséum for a number of years.

Puxton & Worle Station. At one time there was a lot of milk traffic here.

St Anne's Park Station was on the original GWR main line from Paddington. Notice the castellated entrance to the short tunnel east of the station.

ST ANN'S PARK STATION.

Limpley Stoke Station was the junction for Camerton and Hallatrow in the early 1900s.

Line/service	**GWR West of England main line**

Stations closed	*Date*
Langport East	10 September 1962
Long Sutton & Pitney *	10 September 1962
Somerton	10 September 1962
Charlton Mackrell	10 September 1962
Keinton Mandeville	10 September 1962
Alford Halt	10 September 1962
Witham (Somerset) **	3 October 1966

Langport East Station was on the new West of England main line and opened in July 1906.

* Known as Long Sutton & Pitney Halt until 6 April 1908.

** Known as Witham until 9 June 1958.

Railmotor no. 15 at Somerton Station. The power unit was built by Kerr Stuart in 1905. This appears to be a special event, perhaps the inauguration of the railmotor service. No. 15 was withdrawn in 1920, but saw further service on the Nidd Valley Light Railway in Yorkshire.

Keinton Mandeville Station opened in July 1905.

Line/service	**Castle Cary to Yeovil**	*Stations closed*	*Date*
		Sparkford	3 October 1966
		Marston Magna	3 October 1966

Sparkford Station. The ornate cast iron structure on the left was the Gents!

* Known as Marston until 9 May 1895.